C000089584

THE BLACK HUSSARS

A Brief and Concise History of Frederick Diemar's Hussars

Dr. Gary Corrado

No. 1
FOR KING AND COUNTRY
The History of Loyalist Units
During the American Revolution

HERITAGE BOOKS
2011

HERITAGE BOOKS
AN IMPRINT OF HERITAGE BOOKS, INC.

Books, CDs, and more—Worldwide

For our listing of thousands of titles see our website
at
www.HeritageBooks.com

Published 2011 by
HERITAGE BOOKS, INC.
Publishing Division
100 Railroad Ave. #104
Westminster, Maryland 21157

Copyright © 1999 Dr. Gary Corrado

Originally published: Oneonta, New York
Book Lady Publications
1999

Illustration by Thomas Payton

All rights reserved. No part of this book may be reproduced or
transmitted in any form or by any means, electronic or mechanical,
including photocopying, recording or by any information storage
and retrieval system without written permission from the author,
except for the inclusion of brief quotations in a review.

International Standard Book Numbers
Paperbound: 978-0-7884-3540-9
Clothbound: 978-0-7884-8784-2

When revolution broke out across the American colonies, the British government believed it would be a short-lived event, at best. But as the short-lived uprising turned into a full-blown revolution, it soon became apparent the troops already dispatched to the upstart colonies would have to be reinforced by a more mobile force.

Initially, only two regiments of regular dragoons had been sent from England, the 16th and 17th, to help bring the unruly colonists back into line. But, as the American Revolution dragged on, the British high command realized that the vast territories of the colonies required more mounted troops than the regular army could provide. The infantry of the British army could not be expected to traverse wide expanses of constantly changing landscape to capture an elusive Patriot army that had the capability to melt away into the countryside. The army required its eyes, the cavalry, to bring back intelligence reports of the whereabouts and disposition of American troops. They were also needed to provide a messenger service overland between commanders. They were soon to realize that the requirements for cavalry far exceeded their expectations.

Therefore, in 1778 the 16th regiment was disbanded and its men transferred to the 17th regiment. The officers of the 16th were sent back to England to recruit new men to fill its depleted ranks. It did not take long, however, before the British made up the shortage by raising Provincial troops of light dragoons, either as independent troops for attachment to Provincial regiments or as additions to existent regiments.

Captain Diemar's Troop of Hussars was one such troop. Raised in 1779, they were composed of escaped German prisoners of war from the various Brunswick regiments that had

5

accompanied Burgoyne on his ill-fated attempt to split the colonies in two. Having made their way back to New York, and without their officers, these men had become somewhat unruly, so the concept of an independent troop on outpost duty appealed to their instincts.

What made this troop unusual was the fact that while being carried on the Provincial establishment as a Loyalist corps, most of the men were not American, but were in fact Germans. What further distinguished this corps was the fact that they were dressed as hussars. This type of dress in the British army was very new, although the Prussian cavalry had hussar troops for some time. The duty of the hussars, in general, was to be dressed lightly on fast moving horses to provide the quickest mode of communication, as well as to act as the flashing spearhead of an infantry corps. In every battle there exits the moment when the tides can turn. The sudden intervention of a well-trained cavalry corps could well decide the fate of the army. Their mode of attack was lightning-fast, inflicting as much damage on the enemy at that right moment.

Frederick de Diemar held a Captain's commission in the 60th Regiment of Foot, otherwise known as the Royal American Regiment. Upon the recommendation of Prince Ferdinand of Brunswick, Diemar assumed command of the troop in 1779. Fifty-six men, the majority in their early twenties, took the oath of office from Justice of the Peace, his Honor William Waddell. The oath of one such trooper, preserved, reads as follows:

"I, William Waddell, one of His Majesties Justices of the Peace for City and County of New York, do hereby certify that Peter Laughhard, born in the county of Hanover in Germany, aged 20 years, is duly enlisted as a private soldier in the corps styled the Hussars-in His majesty's service under the command of Captain Diemar-that I administered to him the oath of fidelity and that- the 2nd and 6th sections of the articles of war against mutiny and desertion were read to him and he made oath that he does not belong to any of His Majesty's ships or to the marine service."[1]

---

[1] Constance Sherman, "Captain Diemar's Regiment of Hussars on Long Island," *Journal of Long Island History* (summer 1965), 2.

This oath is interesting as it is a complete example of the many oaths generally administered to the Provincial recruits upon their joining the various Loyalist regiments during the war. The total number of men enlisted over the three-year period totaled 180 men.

Diemar and his troop of hussars found themselves attached to Provincial regiments, including Tarleton's Legion and the Queen's Rangers, during various campaigns. The Rangers also had a Hussar company, and given the fact that the Black Hussars, as they were to become known,[2] spent much of their time with, and eventually were joined to the Rangers, their dress was similar. A watercolor, painted by Ranger officer Captain James Murray, of a Hussar private of the Rangers gives us an excellent source of how the troops of Diemar's Hussars were uniformed.[3] The private depicted is wearing a hussar-type cap, with the crescent or half-moon insignia of the Rangers mounted on front, a green wool jacket or short coat, green trousers tucked into short boots, and a sword belt over his right shoulder. His pistol buckets, with bearskin covers, are mounted in front of the saddle. The green saddle blanket has white half-moons on each corner. The diary of Queens Ranger hussar Stephen Jarvis of Stamford, Connecticut described a portmanteau (or valise) mounted on the back of the saddles. Combined with the clothing returns and a list of articles lost by Diemar's troop in a fire in New York, an accurate picture of the Diemar's Hussars' dress can be formulated.[4] The men wore a hussar cap and black coat with blue trousers and boots of the hussar style, that is a short boot with the trousers worn tucked in similar to the Queens Ranger Hussar pictured in the painting. The hussar jacket was probably of a style similar to the Prussian hussar style.[5] They also mounted pistol buckets, but interestingly only one pistol per man was allotted instead of two. This apparent shortage can be explained by Simcoe's assertion in his journal that pistols

---

[2] Philip Katcher, *Encyclopedia of British, Provincial, and German Army Units*, 85.

[3] This painting hangs in the Toronto Metropolitan Library, Toronto, Canada.

[4] See Appendix D.

[5] Diemar Papers, Collections of the Long Island Historical Society, Brooklyn, New York.

were in short supply and he outfitted his troop with such pistols "as could be bought or taken from the enemy." The hussars also wore a broad sword and belt. The broad sword was generally a straight-bladed weapon, sharpened on both edges and designed for hacking the enemy to death. Apparently half the troop was armed with muskets and bayonets and the other half with carbines and carbine belts. This also can be attributed to a shortage of carbines that hampered both sides during the war. The deficiency was made up by regular muskets, which served a double purpose in that they could be used for guard duty when in camp. A dragoon corps without muskets or carbines would not have had much of a chance against attack by an enemy armed with muskets and bayonets, as the 3rd Continental Dragoons found out, much to their chagrin at Old Tappen in New Jersey in September of 1778.[6] All of Diemar's men also wore a cartridge pouch, probably of the waist box variety with the box resting directly on their stomachs and belted around their waists. The information is doubly important for it gives an example of what equipment was issued by the Office of Provincial stores to those troops on the Loyalist establishment. It is logical, therefore, that one can safely conclude the same or similar articles were available to other units as well.

Since Diemar's Hussars were raised primarily for outpost duty, the troop was usually operating on the fringes of British-held territory and would have had a considerable number of skirmishes with the enemy by the very nature of their close proximity. This also meant their duty was quite dangerous and exhausting, exacting a heavy toll on the minds and bodies of the men. Not surprisingly, we find a number of desertions to have taken place over the short history of this corps. Given the international pedigree of the men, from the various provinces of Germany, England, France, America and even Sweden, it is easy to imagine the difficulty of maintaining the discipline of such a corps in a wartime situation.

---

[6] The 3rd Continental Dragoons were also referred to as Lady Washington's Dragoons, as they were often used to accompany Mrs. Washington. Not expecting an attack, they were lightly armed with only with pistols and sabers when they were surprised by the British light infantry, who used their muskets fixed with bayonets as spears giving them a distinct advantage in hand-to-hand combat.

1779

Under ordinary circumstances, a newly formed troop would have had the opportunity to practice drill and maneuvers in order to hone their corps into a well-trained fighting unit. However, this was not the case for the Black Hussars. The troop was immediately thrown into the hornet's nest known then as the neutral territory, or No-Man's land, north of the British lines in New York City. Today we know it as Westchester County, but to the troops on both sides, it was hell on earth. Vigilance and care were exercised by all troops, or the consequences would be severe. Patrols and skirmishes were frequent; rest and relaxation were virtually non-existent. In June the troop marched to North Castle and lost a trooper, probably by desertion.[7]

In mid-July the Hussars participated in the raid on Bedford along with a detachment of 17th dragoons and Tarleton's Legion. The 2nd Continental Dragoons, stationed at Bedford, were so surprised by the violent night-time attack, they lost their regimental standard, and barely had time to mount their horses and flee down the Stamford road ahead of the raiders. Led by Colonel Sheldon, the retreat by the Continentals was made in such a hasty manner that the Stamford Road was derisively called "Sheldon's Race Course" by the local inhabitants for years following the raid.[8] After giving up the chase, Tarleton ordered the village of Bedford burnt because militia snipers continued to fire from the houses, despite repeated warnings by Tarleton to end the practice. Diemar's Hussars only lost one man as a prisoner in this expedition.

In early August, the Hussars accompanied the Queen's Rangers when they overtook an American patrol that had surprised and taken some Westchester Refugees, a Loyalist mounted militia unit, from their quarters. Lt. Colonel John Graves Simcoe,

---

[7] See Appendix E.
[8] Susan Cochran Swanson, *Between the Lines*, 44.

commanding the Queen's Rangers, sent for Tarleton's Legion and Emmerick's Chausseurs to join him in the dash to catch the American patrol. They caught up with them at New Rochelle, freeing many of the Refugee prisoners, and chased the American Col. White of the 4th Continental dragoons away. Simcoe, in his Journal of the Operations of the Queen's Rangers, states:

> "Simcoe...ordered Captain Diemar, who commanded an independent troop of Huzzars, which followed the Queen's Rangers, to pass the wall in pursuit of the enemy's infantry, who had fled from it; he did so; and Captain James, with his troop, and others of the Legion followed him, two or three of whom without orders, and, unsupported, passed the bridge, and were killed there...in the meantime, a Refugee, who had escaped, brought certain intelligence that the enemy were unsupported by any infantry but those with whom the skirmish had happened. One of the enemy was killed by their own fire, close to the fence; two, or three, by Captain Diemar, in the pursuit, others were drowned in passing the creek; and by the enemy's gazette it appeared "that driven into a bad position, they were compelled to fight at a disadvantage, and lost twelve men." The cavalry, on Captain Diemar's return, immediately continued the pursuit to Byre bridge, beyond which it was not prudent or useful to follow: some more of the loyalists were rescued, but none of the enemy overtaken. On the return, the cavalry were divided, by troops, and scoured the woods back to Mamaroneck, but without effect; there they met with the British and Hessian light troops, with whom they returned to camp."[9]

Diemar's Hussars lost one man killed in this skirmish. Simcoe's Journal goes on to state that Diemar's Hussars were placed under his command, and that,

...this whole corps marched for Oyster Bay on the 13th of August: the cavalry, and cannon, by the route of Hell-gates, and the

---

[9] Joan G. Simcoe, *Simcoe's Military Journal*, 105.

infantry by Frog's neck, where they embarked, passed over on the 15th, and joining the cavalry, arrived at Oyster Bay on the 17th."[10]

It appears, however, that some of the Black Hussars remained on outpost duty in Westchester, for three men of the troop deserted from Captain Ferguson's detachment on August 12, and a total of five more deserted during the period of August 24-29 from the outpost at Kingsbridge. Perhaps the combination of the exhausting duty of the previous months, the absence of their commander's presence, and the proximity to the enemy contributed to these sudden desertions. A month later, on September 14, four more members of the Hussars were taken prisoner during a skirmish at Nash's bridge in Westchester while under command of Colonel Tarleton. By October the hazardous campaigns of 1779 had ended for the Hussars when they were sent to winter quarters in the hamlet of Jericho on Long Island with the cavalry of Tarleton and the Queen's Rangers.

---

[10] Ibid., 107.

1780

Diemar's Hussars were transferred to Richmond Town on Staten Island in October 1779 along with the Queens Rangers.[11] Leaving behind trooper John Schulenner, who died at Oyster Bay on February 18, 1780, the troop was posted to the fortifications at Richmond Town in the center of Staten Island, the western-most British-held outpost outside of Manhattan. The British high command believed that if the Americans were to stage a successful attack on the British garrison in New York, Staten Island must fall first. As a result, several British regiments were outposted at various locations on Staten Island. The outpost chosen for the Rangers and Diemar's Hussars was considered the most remote and most susceptible to surprise and capture. Simcoe ordered the Rangers and Hussars to fortify the redoubts by using ingenious traps and ambuscades so that his relatively small force could withstand an attack by a much larger force. He had artillery pieces mounted on sleds for greater mobility in the snow; piles of rocks situated in such locations throughout their field of fire so that a well-place cannon ball amongst them would have the effect of shrapnel; nails place in boards and hidden in the snow on paths most likely to be taken by attacking Americans; a single gunboat frozen in the bay had its cannon piece loaded with grapeshot and aimed at an area where attacking troops would most likely assemble.

While stationed at Richmondtown, the troop participated in several alarms when American troops threatened New York by first landing on Staten Island in January. But the Americans withdrew because of the severity of the weather and preparations made to the fortifications by the Rangers and Hussars. They did not accompany the Legion or Rangers on the expedition to lay siege to Charleston, South Carolina, but remained behind with the Queen's Rangers

---

[11] Simcoe, *Simcoe's Military Journal*, 109.

hussar company under the command of Captain Wickham. However, 51 men of Diemar's troop did make the voyage, not as Hussars, but as returnees to the Hesse-Hanau and Brunswick regiments. Their date of transfer back to their old regiments is recorded as May 15 at the siege of Charleston, though they received their arrears of pay and clothing in the presence of Captain Schlagenteufel at Sandy Hook (New Jersey) on May 19. The captain records that the men were permitted to keep their old breeches and boots as they were mostly *"wore out"* on his Majesty's service.[12]

This transfer of troops may explain why Diemar was only able to muster forty troopers when his unit took part in the raid on Hopper Town (present day Ho-Ho-Kus), New Jersey on April 15. There twenty members of the 17th Dragoons, forty-five troopers of the Queen's Ranger hussars under Captain Wickham, Stuart's Troop of Light Dragoons (Loyalist militia), 300 men of the Regiment De Bose, 100 men of the Regiment von Ditfurth, twelve Jaegers and fifty men of the Loyal American Regiment joined Diemar's Hussars in an attempt to surprise 300 men of the 3rd Pennsylvania Regiment under Colonel Bailey. Captain Diemar's troop followed the advance guard of twelve Queen's Ranger hussars and twelve 17th Light Dragoons into the village. Simcoe recorded the sequence of events:

...Hopper Town is a straggling village, more than a mile long; the farthest house was Colonel Bailey's (real name Byles) quarters; the nearest, a court-house which contained an officer's piquet of twenty men, and which, if properly disposed, covered a bridge over which the troops must pass. The advance was ordered to force the bridge, and to push forward at full speed, through the town, to headquarters: this they effected after receiving an ineffectual fire from the piquet and from some of the windows: the rest of the cavalry dispersed, to pick up the fugitives and to take possession of the rebel's quarters, now abandoned. Cornet Spencer (Q.R.), on his arrival at his post with six men only, the rest not being able to keep up, found about five and twenty men drawn

---

[12] Diemar Papers.

up on the road, opposite him, and divided only by a hollow way and a small brook, with Hopper's house on their right, and a strong fence and swamp on their left. The officer commanding them, whom he afterwards found out to be Bailey (Byles), talked to his men and asked his officers, "Shall we fire now or take possession of the house;" the latter was agreed on. The house was of stone, with three windows below and two above: at the moment of their going in, Cornet Spencer with his party augmented to ten of his own, and by two of the 17th regiment, passed the ravine, and taking possession of the angles of the house, ordered some of his men to dismount and to attempt to force one of the windows. Some servants from a small out-house commenced a fire: Corporal Burt with three men was sent to them, who broke the door open and took nine prisoners. Cornet Spencer made several offers to parley with those who defended head quarters, but to no purpose; they kept up a continual fire: finding it impossible to break the door open, which was attempted, and a man wounded through it, or to force any of the windows, he ordered fire to be brought from the out-house, with which he set fire to one angle of the roof, which was of wood, in flames: he again offered them quarter if they would surrender; they still refused, though the flames were greatly increased. By this time some of the speediest of the cavalry had come to his assistance: the firing ceased. Captains Diemar and Wickham, & c., who had collected a great number of prisoners, and left some few men to guard them, until the infantry should come up, now joined the advance. Col. Bailey (Byles), as he opened the door to surrender, was unfortunately shot by one of Capt. Diemar's huzzars, and died three days after. Of the advance guard two men and three horses were killed, and two men and two horses wounded: and one man and one horse of the 17th regiment were also killed. In this house Col. Bailey, two captains, three subalterns, and twenty-one soldiers were taken. In the whole, twelve officers, with one hundred and eighty-two men were made prisoners. The plan of this expedition was well laid, and as well executed: Major Du Buy seemed to be master of the country through which he had to pass, and was well seconded by Capt. Diemar. Major Du Buy was pleased to honor the huzzars of the Rangers with his particular thanks and approbation. The house *was well defended, and the death of the gallant Colonel Bailey (Byles) was very much regretted by his opponents.*[13]

The Hussars suffered two men and one horse wounded, according to an account published in the Royal Gazette on April 19.

While Sir Henry Clinton was away from New York, supervising the siege of Charleston, South Carolina, General Knyphausen was in temporary command of the New York garrison. The Prussian General had intelligence through one of his aides indicating American morale was low. The Americans were dispirited, not only because the war was dragging on far beyond their expectations, but they also had not received pay. A hand full of their comrades from the Connecticut Continental Line had mutinied in Morristown earlier in the year, May 25, 1780. Refusing to leave the parade ground after muster, an officer was stabbed when he tried to take weapons from his men.[14]

Attempting to take advantage of this situation, and in light of the fact that he also had intelligence indicating local Loyalists had been looking for an excuse to rise up and support the British cause, Knyphausen ordered a mixed force of 5,000 British, German and Loyalist troops, including the Queen's Ranger Hussars and Diemar's Hussars, to push through Elizabethtown and into Connecticut Farms on June 7, to engage Continental troops from New Jersey and Rhode Island, as well as local militia. A series of effectual delaying actions halted the advance. Knyphausen's force retreated back to their beachhead at De Hart's Point where they awaited reinforcements from the fleet returning from the capture of Charleston. During this waiting period one man of Diemar's Hussars deserted, an omen of events to come.

Following the reinforcement, a second raid was conducted with similar results. After this setback, the Queen's Rangers and Diemar's troopers were put on transports and sent up the Hudson River to Westchester County and their old place of the year before in front of the British lines. Once again on outpost duty the

---

[13] Simcoe, *Simcoe's Military Journal*, 141-142.

[14] Christopher Ward, *The War of the Revolution*, 621.

temptation may have been too great, or perhaps sick of all the campaigning or afraid they would all be sent back to the rigid discipline of the German corps, as in the case of fifty-one of their former comrades, thirteen Black Hussars deserted, en masse, from the outpost at Miles Square on July 6. Possibly because of this desertion, the Hussars accompanied the Queen's Rangers to Long Island on July 19, never to see Westchester again.

Diemar's troopers, along with the Queen's Rangers, were stationed on Long Island to secure communications with the British fleet, now off the easternmost tip of the island, and headquarters in New York City. A planned invasion of Rhode Island never materialized, and the corps returned to Oyster Bay on August 23, 1780. During this period Captain Diemar suffered a dangerous fall while carrying dispatches to Sir Henry Clinton. He complained, as late as 1786, the fall had impaired his health[15]. Several members of the troop died at various outposts on Long Island, such as the "*Branch*" (present day Smithtown) in September and December. Apparently this was their winter quarters, for another trooper is recorded as having died in January 1781 at "*Neweltryk, Long Island.*"

In December of 1780, while the Black Hussars remained in winter quarters on Long Island, General Clinton issued orders for another troop of light dragoons to be added to the Queen's Rangers. On December 11, 1780, Lieutenant Cooke of the 17th Light Dragoons was promoted to Captain and placed in command of the new troop.[16] With orders to recruit men, Captain Cooke was left behind as the rest of the Queen's Rangers boarded transports bound for Virginia under the command of the American turncoat-general, Benedict Arnold. Both orders were issued on the same day.

---

[15] Diemar Papers.
[16] Simcoe, *Simcoe's Military Journal*, 159.

1781

Aside from the recorded death of the trooper in January, no further mention of the Black Hussars is made until April 24 when they were merged into the troop being raised by Captain Cooke. Sixty-two men of that unique corps would now wear the green coats of the celebrated Queen's Rangers, not as hussars, but as the new Light Dragoons. Their dress was to be similar to Tarleton's dragoons, though when they first reported to their regiment down south, on May 28, they arrived *"without a single cavalry, appointment, or arms."*[17] Simcoe relates that the arms and accoutrements which were intended for Captain Cooke's troop, were sent by the Inspector to Lord Cornwallis, who in turn gave them to Tarleton's dragoons. The troop was not present at the surrender of the Queen's Rangers at Yorktown in October; rather they were detached for patrol duty with other troops of Queen's Rangers dragoons in the Charleston, South Carolina, area.

---

[17] Ibid., 211.

EPILOGUE

Thus ended the military history of Diemar's Hussars, a curious footnote to the campaigns of the Revolutionary War. Their service did not cause any changes in the conduct of the war, nor did they particularly distinguish themselves in anything but skirmishes and patrol duty. However, their service was important in that it provided a mobile strike force and reconnaissance for the British army, a duty they performed well. Captain Frederick de Diemar rejoined his 60th Regiment, and as late as 1790 offered his services to raise a third battalion of the regiment.

APPENDIX A

RETURN OF STORES BURNT AT THE FIRE THE 20TH OF NOV. 1780 AND BELONGING TO THE TROOP OF HUSSARS

1	Chest with 3 pieces of blue cloth, 1 piece of green cloth, 2 pieces of white and 1 piece of red flannel
22	New blankets and 6 blankets, already used
3	Hussar jackets
3	Blue great cloaks
4	Blue trousers
4	pair white breeches
2	pair boots
2	pair of Soleleders
24	carabines
27	muskets and bayonets
65	cartridge boxes
2	carabine belts
2	swords
4	saddles, 4 bridles, and 4 pair of pistols
24	canteens
1	Bugle horn
1	Bellis
1	Hussar cap
1	pair spurs
8	pair of curry combs and brushes
1	chest belonging to Lt. Albus

Sergeant Leibert lost:

1	a great coat
1	blue trowser
1	pair of boots
2	pair stockings
1	white jacket
1	pair spurs
1	shirt

Mrs. Leibert lost at the fire:

1	a head
2	long gowns
2	shirts
1	coffee kettle
1	pair stockings
2	black silk handkerchiefs

19

APPENDIX B

ARTICLES OF CLOTHING RECEIVED, LOST AND WANTED –
September 10, 1779

ARTICLE	RECEIVED	LOST	WANTING TO COMPLETE
Sergeants suits	2	1	2
Trumpeters black coat	2	1	
Trumpeter's Waistcoat	1		
Black coats	50	9	16
Buff coats	54	9	12
Pairs Trousers	54	9	12
Pairs boots	66	9	
Saddles complete	55	9	11
Broadswords	57	9	9
Trumpet	1		
Pistols	38	7	28
Blankets	56	9	10
Camp Kettles	6		
Pouches	8		
Buckets	56	9	
Sword belts and lips	66		

60 canteens are wanting and one picket line.

Signed Frederick de Diemar
Captain 60th R.

APPENDIX C

A LIST OF ARTICLES SUPPLIED TO THE HUSSARS BY THE OFFICE OF
PROVINCIALS AND THOSE STILL LACKING, OCTOBER 2, 1779

ITEM	RECEIVED	LOST BY DESERTION OF PRISONERS	REMAINING OCT. 2	WANTING TO COMPLETE TROOP
Caps	60	-	60	2
Shirts	-	-	-	62
Coats	57	13	44	19 (sic)
Waistcoats	56	13	43	19
Trousers	-	13	43	19
Camp Kettles	-	-	6	6
Blankets	56	13	43	19
Pouches	56	13	43	19
Tents	-	-	-	12
Saddles (Complete)	55	13	42	20
Spurs	56	-	56	6
Pistols	38	13	25	37
Broadswords	57	13	44	18
Sword Belts and Lips	66	13	53	9
Forage Cords	-	-	-	1
Picket Line	-	-	-	-
Trumpets	1	-	-	1
Boots, (pairs)	66	13	53	62
Troop consists of 62 men	62	1	1	62

APPENDIX D

ABSTRACTS
OF
DIEMAR'S CLAIMS TO ENGLAND

No. 8   94 wooden canteens

No. 11   Captain Saunders, Queens Rangers Certificate for 62
         men for which no more but 3 guineas bounty money
         had been allowed to Capt. Diemar, although they were
         raised at 6, 7, and 8 guineas to secure him the same
         royal favor as has been granted to all other Provincial
         Commanders

No. 14   Payment for four Pike Axes to Mr. Bruff, Sword
         Cutter at New York- used in the 1779 on the
         expedition to Virginia by B. General Clarke - certificate

APPENDIX E

ROSTER OF THE HUSSAR CORPS RAISED BY CAPTAIN FREDERICK de DIEMAR 1779-1781

1. Ahrens, Henry, Private, enlisted May 16, 1779; returned to the Brunswick corps May 15, 1780
2. Alberty, Charles, of Brunswick, age 22, Private. Enlisted April 13, 1779; deserted from Captain Ferguson's detachment August 12, 1779
3. Albright, James, of Germany, age 27, Private. Enlisted November 6, 1780; delivered Queen's Rangers dragoons April 24, 1781
4. Albus, George, Lieutenant, enlisted April 11, 1779; remained in Queen's Rangers
5. Alter, William, of Hesse Hanover, age 24, Private. Enlisted July 29, 1779; returned to the Hesse Hanau corps May 15, 1780
6. Baling, John Henry, of Bremen, age 24, Private. Enlisted September 22, 1779; returned to the Brunswick corps Oct. 15, 1779 (?) (February 24 or May 15, 1780)
7. Barns, John, of Hanover, age 34, Private. Enlisted October 5, 1780; delivered Queen's Rangers dragoons April 24, 1781
8. Barth, Caspar (Bart, Henry) of Pennsylvania, age 17, Private and Corporal. Enlisted June 25, 1780; delivered Queen's Rangers dragoons April 24, 1781
9. Baseke (Baeseke), Frederick, Private. Enlisted April 8, 1779; returned wounded to the Brunswick corps May 15, 1780
10. Becker, Christian, of Brunswick, age 20, Private and Corporal. Enlisted July 29, 1779; delivered Queen's Rangers dragoons April 24, 1781
11. Benneroth, Henry, Corporal. Enlisted April 8, 1779; returned to the Brunswick corps May 15, 1780
12. Berg, John (Philip) of Hesse Hanau, age 23, Private. Enlisted December 23, 1780; delivered Queen's Rangers dragoons April 24, 1781

13. Berkner, Joseph, Private. Enlisted April 8, 1779; killed in the skirmish at New Rochelle August 7, 1779

14. Bilsingsteben, Ensign Charles von, Private. Enlisted July 26, 1780; delivered Queen's Rangers dragoons April 24, 1781

15. Bodenstein, Frederick of Brunswick age 22, Private. Enlisted July 29, 1779; delivered Queen's Rangers dragoons April 24, 1781

16. Bofse, Henry, Private. Enlisted July 29, 1779; taken prisoner at Nash's Bridge under Tarleton September 14, 1779

17. Bohm, Henry, Private. Enlisted July 29 (or August 12) 1779; returned to the Brunswick troops May 15, 1780

18. Bohmer (Boehmer, Boehm), Henry (John), of Brunswick, age 28, Private. Enlisted January 19 (17), 1781; delivered Queen's Rangers dragoons April 24, 1781

19. Bonnblush, John, Private. Enlisted March 23, 1779; taken prisoner at Nash's Bridge under Tarleton September 14, 1779

20. Bontems, Guillame, Private. Enlisted May 18, 1780; delivered Queen's Rangers dragoons April 24, 1781

21. Bornemann (Bourman), George, Private. Enlisted May 16, 1780; delivered Queen's Rangers dragoons April 24, 1781

22. Braumann, John, Private. Enlisted July 29 (or April 8) 1779; returned to the Brunswick troops May 15, 1780

23. Brinckmann, Charles (Diedrich), Private. Enlisted August 12, 1779; returned to the Brunswick corps May 15, 1780

24. Brown, Charles (Yorke), Private. Enlisted March 14, 1779; discharged as a batman April 24, 1781

25. Brown (Browne), James, of Middlesex, England, age 21, Private. Enlisted November 6, 1780, delivered Queen's Rangers dragoons April 24, 1781

26. Brunau, William de, Private. Enlisted March 2, 1780; deserted advance post Miles Square July 6, 1780

27. Burmann (Boarman), Henry (George), Farrier and Private. Enlisted October 5, 1779; delivered Queen's Rangers dragoons April 24, 1781 (discharged May 15, 1780)

28. Buther, Henry, of Hanover, age 29. Private. Enlisted June 16, 1779; returned to the Navy by order July 1, 1780 (June 24, 1779)

29. Campen, Henry, of Hanover, age 21, Private. Enlisted November 18, 1780; delivered to Captain Ottendorff by orders from Headquarters November 29, 1780

30. Carle (Charl), Ferdinand (Gerd), of Hanover, age 48, Private. Enlisted May 14, 1779; discharged as a servant December 24, 1780.

31. Castelbeyn (Haslinbien), Christian, Private. Enlisted April 8, 1779; returned to the Brunswick corps May 15, 1780

32. Chevalier, Gabriel, of Geneva, age 23, Private. Enlisted February 18, 1780; deserted advance post, Miles Square, July 6, 1780

33. Christian, Frederick, Private. Enlisted October 6, 1780; delivered Queen's Rangers dragoons April 24, 1781

34. Christian, Lars (Sass), Private, Enlisted July 1, 1780, deserted General Hospital, New York, December 21, 1780

35. Christian, Neals, Private, Enlisted July 15, 1780; died at the Branch on Long Island, September 27, 1780

36. Clammer, Daniel, Private, Enlisted July 6, 1780; delivered Queen's Rangers dragoons April 24, 1781

37. Cruckmyer (Crickamyer), Henry, of Pennsylvania, age 20, Private. Enlisted December 23, 1780; delivered Queen's Rangers dragoons April 24, 1781

38. Curdmann, Henry, Private. Enlisted April 8, 1779; returned to the Brunswick troops May 15, 1780

39. Curs, Christopher, Private, Enlisted April 8, 1779; returned to the Brunswick corps May 15, 1780

40. Curs (Cours), Frederick, Private. Enlisted October 16, 1779; returned to the Brunswick corps May 15, 1780

41. Daniel, John, Private. Enlisted May 2,1780; returned to Captain Lavid of the Navy June 23, 1780

42. Dieffenbach (Diffenback), Christoph, Private. Enlisted December 27, 1779; returned to the Hessians by order May 9, 1780

43. Diemar, Ferdinand de, Volunteer. Enlisted December 23, 1780; joined Third Battalion, Sixtieth Regiment April 24, 1781

44. Diemar, Frederick de, Captain Sixtieth Regiment. Enlisted April 11, 1779; ordered to rejoin the 60th April 24, 1781; Sold troop to Queen's Rangers same day

45. Diemar, Julius de, Volunteer. Enlisted December 23, 1780; joined Loyal American Regiment April 24, 1781

46. Dietmer (Ditmer, Delmer), John, of Hamburg, age 23, Private, Corporal, and Sergeant. Enlisted June 12, 1779; delivered Queen's Rangers dragoons April 24, 1781

47. Dittfurth (Ditfurth, Derford), Lieutenant Lewis de, of Hesse, age 29, Volunteer. Enlisted May 16 (18), 1780, delivered April 24, 1781

48. Dralle, Henry, of Brunswick, age 22, Private. Enlisted July 29, 1779; taken prisoner at Nash's Bridge under Tarleton September 14, 1779 (discharged May 15, 1780)

49. Drecksel (Drechsel), Frederick, of the County of Anspach, age 21, Private. Enlisted October 2, 1779; returned to the Brunswick corps May 15, 1780

50. Drings (Dinges), John (Andreas, Adam), of Brunswick, age 19, Private. Enlisted 8, 1779; missing on the march to North Castle June 12, 1779

51. Dufour, Joseph, Private and Corporal. Enlisted February 18, 1780; deserted advance post, Miles Square, July 6, 1780

52. Ehrhard, John, Private. Enlisted October 1, 1780; delivered Queen's Rangers, April 24, 1781

53. Ely, Peter, Private. Enlisted May 18, 1780; delivered Queen's Rangers, April 24, 1781

54. Erron, Pierre, Private. Enlisted May 18, 1780, deserted New York June 8, 1780

55. Faulstroh, Henry, Trumpeter. Enlisted April 8, 1779; returned to the Hesse Hanau Corps May 15, 1780

56. Ferdris, Chris (John) of Brunswick, age 20, Private. Enlisted October 2, 1779; returned to the Brunswick Corps May 15, 1780

57. Fink, Michael, of Philadelphia, age 22, Private. Enlisted November 6, 1780; died outpost Neweltryk, on Long Island, January 22 (27), 1781

58. Fittler, Andrew (Andreas), of Brunswick, age 23, Private. Enlisted July 29, 1779; returned to the Brunswick Corps May 15, 1780
59. Franciscus, George, Private. Enlisted April 13, 1779; returned to the Hessians by order May 19, 1779, though another record states he was discharged June 28, 1780
60. Frey, Christoph, Trumpeter, Private. Enlisted October 8 (25), 1779; delivered Queen's Rangers April 24, 1781
61. Frey (Fry), Joseph, of Hampshire, England, age 32, Private. Enlisted July 15, 1780; delivered Queen's Rangers troop April 24, 1781
62. Forrester, Samuel, Private. Enlisted July 15, 1780; delivered Queen's Rangers troop April 24, 1781
63. Frehling, Lewis (Fruling, Ludwig), Farrier and Private. Enlisted April 8, 1779; returned to the Brunswick Corps May 15, 1780
64. Gehrke (Gercke), Henry, of Lunenberg, age 22, Private. Enlisted July 5, 1779; deserted advance post Miles Square, July 6, 1780
65. Goetz, Jacob, Private. Enlisted August 12, 1779; returned to the Brunswick Corps December 19, 1779 (May 15, 1780)
66. Gofsis, John, Private. Enlisted July 3, 1779; deserted from Captain Ferguson's detachment August 25, 1779
67. Griffiths, Richard, Volunteer and Quartermaster. Enlisted February 24, 1780; died New York 1781
68. Grote (Grothe), John, of Hanover, age 42, Private. Enlisted October 3, 1780; discharged as a servant February 24, 1781
69. Grunberg, Christian, Private. Enlisted July 7, 1780; deserted General Hospital, New York, January 18, 1781
70. Grundlach (Gundelach), Christ, Private. Enlisted April 8, 1779; returned to the Brunswick Corps May 15, 1780
71. Gunn, George, Private. Enlisted October 26, 1780; delivered 43rd Regiment February 24, 1781
72. Haase, Henry, of Brunswick, age 21, private. Enlisted July 29, 1779; returned to the Brunswick troops May 15, 1780
73. Hallmann, Henry, Private. Enlisted December 23, 1780; died General Hospital, New York, April 15, 1781

74. Handel (Handell, Hanlon), Edward, of Dublin, age 22, Private. Enlisted July 15, 1780; delivered Queen's Rangers troop April 24, 1781

75. Hanning, Barry, Private. Enlisted July 15, 1780; Queen's Rangers troop April 24, 1781

76. Haumann, John, Sergeant and Quartermaster, Enlisted July 29, 1779; taken prisoner on the march to Bedford July 14, 1779. Returned to the Brunswick troops May 15, 1780

77. Hendricks, Hans, Private. Enlisted August 3, 1780; delivered Queen's Rangers troop April 24, 1781

78. Herring, Charles, of Hesse Cassel, age 43, Private. Enlisted October 19, 1779; delivered Queen's Rangers troop April 24, 1781 (May 15, 1780)

79. Heye, Conrad, of Germany, age 22, Private. Enlisted May 21, 1780; deserted advance post, Miles Square, July 6, 1780

80. Hohendorff, Lieutenant Frederick de, Sergeant. Enlisted December 23, 1780; delivered Queen's Rangers April 24, 1781

81. Hoppe, John, Private. Enlisted April 8, 1779; returned to the Brunswick troops May 15, 1780

82. Horn, Godfrey, Private. Enlisted July 1, 1780; delivered Queen's Rangers troop April 24, 1780

83. Horn, Lewis (Ludwig), Private. Enlisted April 8, 1779; delivered Queen's Rangers troop April 24, 1781

84. Howard, Charles, of Sweden, age 35, Private. Enlisted July 7, 1780; delivered Queen's Rangers troop April 24, 1781

85. Huchthausen (Uhrausen), Henry (George), Private. Enlisted October 5, 1779; returned to the Brunswick Corps May 15, 1780

86. Humpff, (Stumph), John, Private. Enlisted 12, 1780, delivered Queen's Rangers troop April 24, 1781

87. Ianeke, Henry, Private. Enlisted May 18, 1779; returned to the Navy by order September 2, 1779.

88. Ifland, John [Heinman], Private. Enlisted April 8, 1779; returned to the Hesse Hanau Corps May 15, 1780.

89. Jansen, [Johnson], Conrad, of Brunswick, age 38, Private. Enlisted July 29, 1779; returned to the Brunswick Troops May 15, 1780.

90. Jessen, Peter, Private. Enlisted July 10, 1780; delivered Queen's Rangers troop April 24, 1781

91. Johannson (Johanson, Uhanssan), Uhly (Ohle), of Sweden, age 30, Private. Enlisted July 1, 1780; delivered Queen's Rangers troop April 24, 1781

92. Johnson, Christian, Private. Enlisted July 18, 1780; impressed by the Navy on board the Sandwich December 19, 1780

93. Juliat, Lieutenant, Henry, Private and Corporal. Enlisted June 24, 1780; discharged at the request of His Serene Highness of Palatine, February 24, 1781

94. Kael, Jeremiah, Private. Enlisted December 23, 1780; delivered to the Queen's Rangers troop April 24, 1781

95. Karz, Peter, County of Pennsylvania. Age 29, Private. Enlisted May 21, 1780; delivered Queen's Rangers troop April 24, 1781

96. Kayser (Keyser), Frederick, Private. Enlisted May 19, 1779; delivered Queen's Rangers troop April 24, 1781

97. Keydel (Keydell), John, Private. Enlisted May 23, 1780; delivered Queen's Rangers troop April 24, 1781

98. Kinner, John, Private. Enlisted March 25, 1781; delivered Queen's Rangers troop April 24, 1781

99. Knigge, Christian, Private. Enlisted May 19, 1779; returned to the Brunswick Corps May 15, 1780

100. Knyrean, Lewis, Private. Enlisted October 16, 1779; returned to the Brunswick Corps May 15, 1780

101. Kolemann, Alexander (Collman), Private. Enlisted April 11, 1779; discharged as a servant June 28, 1779

102. La Feuillade (La Fayette), Lewis, Private. Enlisted May 18, 1780; delivered Queen's Rangers troop April 24, 1781

103. Langeludeke, Henry (John), Private. Enlisted April 8, 1779; deserted outpost, Kingsbridge, August 29, 1779

104. Laughhard, (Lauckhart), Private. Enlisted July 29, 1779; returned to the Hesse Hanau Corps May 15, 1780

105. Le Blanc (Blanc), Andrew, France, Age 27, Private. Enlisted May 16, 1780; deserted advance post, Miles Square, July 6, 1780

106. Levy, Joseph, Private. Enlisted March 14, 1779. Deserted advance post, Miles Square, July 6, 1780

107. Littman (Lietman), John (George), Private. Enlisted September 21, 1779; returned to the Brunswick Corps May 15, 1780

108. Lohmann, Henry (Lohmanns), Private. Enlisted April 1, 1780; deserted advance post Miles Square, July 6, 1780

109. Luger, Christopher, age 30, Private. Enlisted June 1, 1779; delivered Queen's Rangers troop April 24, 1781

110. Lund, Jacob, Private. Enlisted July 1, 1780 ; delivered Queen's Rangers troop April 24, 1781

111. Maas (Moss), C. Anthony, of Germany, age 28, Private. Enlisted October 1, 1780; delivered Queen's Rangers troop April 24, 1781

112. Marmillon (Marmelon, Milton), George (Francois), of France, age 20, Private. Enlisted December 23, 1780; delivered Queen's Rangers troop April 24, 1781

113. Marsh, (Mash), Andrew, of Frankfurt, age 31, Private. Enlisted July 1, 1779; deserted outpost Kingsbridge, October 24, 1779

114. Martin, Jean, Private. Enlisted October 9, 1780; delivered Queen's Rangers troop April 24, 1781

115. Meisner, August, Private. Enlisted October 8, 1779; returned to the Brunswick Corps May 15, 1780

116. Miller, John, Private. Enlisted October 26, 1780; delivered 43rd Regiment of Foot, February 24, 1781

117. Miller, Lewis, of Prussia, age 44, Corporal and Sergeant. Enlisted April 4, 1779; delivered Queen's Rangers troop April 24, 1781

118. Molitor, Lieutenant Sebastion de. Enlisted April 11, 1779; put on half pay April 24, 1781

119. Moor, Phillip, Private. Enlisted July 5, 1779; deserted from Captain Ferguson's detachment August 25, 1779

120. Moorshel, John, Sergeant and Quartermaster. Enlisted July 29, 1779; returned to the Hesse Hanau Corps April 24, 1780 (May 15, 1780)

121. Mueller, Christian (Francis), Private. Enlisted August 12, 1779; returned to the Brunswick Corps May 15, 1780

122. Mueller, Christoph, Private. Enlisted May 19, 1779; returned to the Brunswick Corps May 15, 1780

123. Mushard (Moschert), Christian, of Hamburg, age 23, Private. Enlisted June 12, 1779; deserted Headquarters, New York, January 10, 1781

124. Myer, Charles (William), Corporal. Enlisted April 4, 1779; delivered Queen's Rangers troop April 24, 1781

125. Myer, Christoph (Christian), of Hungary, age 25, Private. Enlisted October 25, 1779; deserted advance post Miles Square, July 6, 1780

126. Myer, Marius, Private. Enlisted June 25, 1780; returned to the Hessians December 24, 1780

127. Pactsch, Georg, Private. Enlisted June 25, 1780; died at The Branch on Long Island September 30, 1780

128. Page, William, Private. Enlisted February 2, 1780 (oath administered by Henry Hewlett February 7, 1780); delivered Queen's Rangers troop April 24, 1781

129. Papineau, Lewis, Private. Enlisted October 10, 1780; delivered Queen's Rangers troop April 24, 1781

130. Pennys, Charles, Private. Enlisted January 10, 1781; delivered Queen's Rangers troop April 24, 1781

131. Perry (Berry), Richard, of Yorkshire, age 26, Private. Enlisted November 6, 1780; delivered Queen's Rangers troop April 24, 1781

132. Peter, John, Private. Enlisted July 4, 1780; delivered Queen's Rangers troop April 24, 1781

133. Petors, John, Private. Enlisted August 2, 1780; delivered Queen's Rangers troop April 24, 1781

134. Plate (Platt, Plat), John, of Hanover, age 28, Private. Enlisted July 10, 1780; delivered Queen's Rangers troop April 24, 1781

135. Probst, Henry (John), Private and Corporal. Enlisted April 8, 1779; returned to the Brunswick Corps May 15, 1780

136. Raabe, Nicolaus (Nicholas), of Hamburg, age 28, Private. Enlisted May 30, 1779; delivered Queen's Rangers troop April 24, 1781

137. Radichel (Radifichell), Chris, Sergeant and Saddler, Brunswick staff; Enlisted April 8, 1779; returned to the Brunswick Corps May 15, 1780

138. Rampendahl, Frederick, Surgeon's Mate. Enlisted May 16, 1779; discharged by the Inspector General April 24, 1781

139. Rapp, Peter, Private. Enlisted April 8, 1779; deserted outpost Kingsbridge, October 26, 1779

140. Raschorn, Christian, Private. Enlisted May 19, 1779; returned to the Brinswick troops May 15, 1779

141. Raschenbach, Christoph, Private and Corporal. Enlisted June 25, 1780; delivered Queen's Rangers troop April 24, 1781

142. Rinne, Lewis, Private. Enlisted August 12, 1779; returned to the Brunswick corps May 15, 1780

143. Rogge, Charles, Private. Enlisted April 8, 1779; returned to the Brunswick troops February 24, 1780 (May 15, 1780)

144. Roggenstadt, Valentine, Private. Enlisted July 1, 1779; deserted outpost Kingsbridge August 29, 1779

145. Rolle (Rohl), Conrad, Private. Enlisted June 14, 1779; died on Long Island November (December) 22, 1780

146. Rumberg, Henry, Private. Enlisted April 8, 1779; returned to the Brunswick troops May 15, 1780

147. Runge, Andrew (George), Private. Enlisted August 12, 1779; returned to the Brunswick corps May 15, 1780

148. Row, John, of Middlesex, age 23. Enlisted March 25, 1781; delivered Queen's Rangers troop April 24, 1781

149. Saggert (Sagart), Christian, Private. Enlisted December 29, 1779; deserted advance post Miles Square, July 6, 1780

150. Samuel, August, Private. Enlisted March 25, 1781; delivered Queen's Rangers troop April 24, 1781

151. Schildenberg, John, Private. Enlisted May 21, 1780; deserted advance post Miles Square July 6, 1780

152. Schlueter (Schlieter), Anthony, Private Enlisted April 8, 1779; returned to the Brunswick troops May 15, 1780

153. Schneider, Henry, Private. Enlisted July 29, 1779; returned to the Hesse Hanau corps May 15, 1780

154. Schroeder (Schroder), Henry, Private. Enlisted June 2, 1779; deserted outpost Kingsbridge, October 24, 1779

155. Schulenner, John, Private. Enlisted April 11, 1779; died at the outpost Oyster Bay, February 18, 1780

156. Schwartz (Swartz), Frederick, Private. Enlisted October 16, 1779; returned to the Brunswick corps May 15, 1780

157. Scyhler, George, Private and Corporal. Enlisted March 14, 1779; deserted East Chester July 12, 1779

158. Seitz (Setz), John C., of Anspach, age 17, Private. Enlisted September 19, 1779; delivered Queen's Rangers troop April 24, 1781

159. Semmell, John, Private. Enlisted April 1, 1780; deserted advance post Miles Square, July 6, 1780

160. Sentzell, John (Sencell, Nicholas), Private. Enlisted April 8, 1779; returned to the Hesse Hanau corps May 15, 1780

161. Shibley, John, Private. Enlisted May 16, 1780; discharged as a servant February 24, 1781

162. Siebert, Lieutenant Henry, of Germany, age 24, Private, Corporal, and Sergeant. Enlisted July 29, 1779; delivered Queen's Rangers troop April 24, 1781

163. Sievert, Peter, Private. Enlisted March 25, 1781; delivered Queen's Rangers troop April 24, 1781

164. Sower, Jacob, Private, Enlisted April 1, 1779; returned to the Brunswick corps February 24, 1780

165. Sower, John, Private. Enlisted April 1, 1779; returned to the Brunswick corps February 24, 1780

166. Spiess (Spees), Henry, of Germany, age 25, Private. Enlisted November 6, 1780; delivered Queen's Rangers troop April 24, 1781

167. Steckham (Stekhane), Gottlieb, of Brunswick, age 22, Private. Enlisted October 1, 1779; returned to the Brunswick corps May 15, 1780

168. Stein (Stone), John, of Exenbergh, age 40, Private. Enlisted January 17, 1780; deserted Camp Elizabeth Town June 13, 1780

169. Suderquest, John, Private, Enlisted July 1, 1780; delivered Queen's Rangers troop April 24, 1781

170. Taubenheim, Frederick, Private, Corporal and Sergeant. Enlisted April 8, 1779; returned to the Brunswick corps December 14, 1780 (May 15, 1780)

171. Thomson, Benjamin, Cornet. Enlisted June 24, 1779; remained in the Queen's Rangers

172. Timme, John, Private. Enlisted April 11, 1779; returned to the Brunswick corps May 15, 1780

173. Titzell (Fitzell), William, Private. Enlisted February 24, 1780; returned to General Knyphausen's regiment May 4, 1780

174. Turnier, Charles (Tournier, George), Private. Enlisted September 21, 1779; returned to the Brunswick corps May 15, 1780

175. Volmer, Gottlieb, of Prussia, age 22, Private. Enlisted April 4, 1779; discharged from the General Hospital July 10, 1779

176. Williams, William, Private. Enlisted July 18, 1780; impressed by the Navy on board the Sandwich December 19, 1780

177. Wilson, John, of York, England, age 22, Private. Enlisted October 18, 1780; delivered Queen's Rangers troop April 24, 1781

178. Wirth, John, Private. Enlisted July 20, 1780; delivered Queen's Rangers troop April 24, 1781

179. Wohls, Emanuel (Wohlls, John), Private. Enlisted August 12, 1779; returned to the Brunswick corps May 15, 1780

180. Zimmerman, Christ (Gottfrid), Private. Enlisted April 8, 1779; taken prisoner at Nash's Bridge under Colonel Tarleton September 14, 1779

BIBLIOGRAPHY

Diemar Papers. Collections of the Long Island Historical Society. Brooklyn, New York.

Katcher, Philip R.N. *Encyclopedia of British, Provincial, and German Army Units.* Harrisburg, PA: Stackpole Books, 1973.

Sherman, Constance. "Captain Diemar's Regiment of Hussars on Long Island." *Journal of Long Island History.* Brooklyn, New York, 1965.

Simcoe, Joan G. *Simcoe's Military Journal.* New York: Bartlett & Welford, 1844.

Swanson, Susan Cochran. *Between the Lines.* Pelham, New York: Junior League of Pelham, 1975.

Ward, Christopher. *The War of the Revolution.* New York: Macmillian Company, 1952.

13181348R00022

Made in the USA
San Bernardino, CA
14 July 2014